THE COMPLETE *DARK SHADOWS* (OF MY CHILDHOOD)

BOOK 1

THE COMPLETE *DARK SHADOWS* (OF MY CHILDHOOD)

BOOK 1

TONY TRIGILIO

BLAZEVOX[BOOKS]
Buffalo, New York

The Complete Dark Shadows (of My Childhood) Book 1
by Tony Trigilio

Copyright © 2014

Published by BlazeVOX [books]

Printed in the United States of America

Interior design and typesetting by Geoffrey Gatza
Cover Design by Michael Trigilio

First Edition
ISBN: 978-1-60964-143-6
Library of Congress Control Number: 2013942424

BlazeVOX [books]
131 Euclid Ave
Kenmore, NY 14217

Editor@blazevox.org

publisher of weird little books

BlazeVOX [books]

blazevox.org

21 20 19 18 17 16 15 14 13 12 01 02 03 04 05 06 07 08 09 10

BlazeVOX

FOR MARGARET TRIGILIO

Table of Contents

The Complete *Dark Shadows*
(of My Childhood)

Book 1

Synopsis

Dark Shadows was a soap opera broadcast weekdays on the ABC television network from 1966-1971. The show set itself apart from other daytime soaps with its relentlessly gothic aesthetic and plot lines built around ghosts and other supernatural phenomena. The uncanny became a permanent feature of *Dark Shadows*. It remains the only haunted soap opera in American TV history.

On April 17, 1967 (Episode 210), the show introduced the character of Barnabas Collins, a vampire from the eighteenth century accidentally freed from his chained coffin in 1967 by a grave robber, Willie Loomis. The show's producers originally intended to keep the Barnabas character around for only a 13-week narrative arc. But he quickly became the most popular character on the show, and he remained a central figure from April 1967 through the show's cancellation in 1971.

Barnabas Collins was the star of nearly all my childhood nightmares. I watched the show every day with my mother, a devoted soap opera fan, in the first months and years of my life—and many of my earliest memories are terrifying recollections of Barnabas stalking me. I was petrified by Barnabas; at the same time, the vampire also was an object of insatiable curiosity for me. My feelings about Barnabas were nurtured and sustained before I came into language, and are twined with some of my most primal sensations.

Production Notes

This is the first book of a multi-volume poem. I intend to watch all 1,225 episodes of *Dark Shadows,* composing one sentence for each episode and shaping the sentences into couplets. Book 1 opens with Episode 210, Barnabas's arrival in Collinsport, Maine, and runs for 183 episodes, ending with Episode 392. The epigraphs at the beginning of each section are taken from the *Dark Shadows* introductory teasers spoken by individual characters in voiceover at the beginning of each episode.

I will return to Episodes 1-209 in the final volume, as a kind of prequel/coda, after I have watched the last episode of the series. The show was preempted 20 times during its five-year run, and in these instances the network double-numbered or triple-numbered the episodes so that the show airing on a Friday would always end in a 5 or a 0. The final episode of *Dark Shadows*, then, is officially Episode 1,245, even though it was actually the 1,225th episode produced for the show.

The author wishes to thank the editors of the following journals and anthologies in which excerpts from this book appeared, often in different versions: *Puerto del Sol; Rabbit Ears: TV Poems; Stolen Island;* and *TriQuarterly.* Huge thanks to Jan Bottiglieri, Geoffrey Gatza, Chris Green, Larry Janowski, Liz Shulman, Michael Trigilio, David Trinidad, and Monica Wilson.

THE COMPLETE *DARK SHADOWS* (OF MY CHILDHOOD)

BOOK 1

1.

Night is drawing nearer and nearer to Collinwood.
Another man has come—a stranger who is not a stranger.

Everyone pushes Willie Loomis around,
like a scarecrow, and he only makes it worse

busting Barnabas Collins from his casket.
That's Barnabas, looking as if he were

alive, posing next to his ancient portrait
at the foot of the stairs. Barnabas Collins,

source of my childhood nightmares, rolls
the "r" in "Victoria" with a lilt, a graceful excess,

prim and courtly and swallowing blood.

_____

Over drinks at The Blue Whale, Burke spends
half an episode apologizing to Carolyn,

who walks out when the samba music starts.
Two great houses in Collinwood, Barnabas

compares one to the pyramids of Egypt:
"The plaster walls were made from crushed

clamshells and horsehair." Joe, distracted
at The Blue Whale, keeps seeing that little calf

drained of his blood (but doesn't seem to notice
the half-shell ashtrays). Don't bring Willie

back to Collinwood to apologize to Carolyn,
Jason, unless you want him to faint when he

sees the 207-year-old vampire's portrait.

_____

Watching three straight episodes with Liz
but Barnabas doesn't appear, and tonight

Jason said "Willie" 33 times (if the writers
don't start giving Barnabas more scenes,

how can I expect her to understand I slept

with my shoulders hunched to ward off

vampires as a child?). Yet another scene
begins with Roger pouring sherry from

the parlor decanter; swishing his lowball glass,
he calls Jason and Willie "sea tramps."

Who on earth writes Victoria's tortured
introductions: here comes a dawn that

"slowly creeps toward Collinwood"
and a man (Willie?) who "emerges from

the darkest pit the night can know"—
who, through the mists, "brings with him

the torments of the night into the day."

———————————————————

"I'll lose everything if I stick with you, kid,"
Jason says with a straight face to Willie,

who disappears into the cemetery at night
and lies in bed tossing and sighing all day

like a nineteenth-century neurasthenic.
Stroking the wolf's-head cane he used

to shatter my bedroom window
in a recurring nightmare, Barnabas jokes

with Maggie about night-time loneliness
and apologizes for striking up a conversation:

flirting, you're doing it wrong, old man.

———————————————————

Standing before a wavy portrait of a man
holding a baby or hugging himself—

each time I rewind, it's something different—
Barnabas asks Maggie's father, Sam,

to paint him by candlelight after sundown
. . . and they can start right now, tonight.

Episode 223, in which Little David,
the psychic child, fumbles his lines

four times in one scene and Elizabeth
Stoddard calls a painting a photograph.

Why is David so scared of the Old House
—he faced down his mother's ghost there,

after all, in a circle of flame, long before
Barnabas rose from the grave.

Maggie doesn't have to make sense
all the time, especially when she dreams

she opened a coffin on a misty plain
and found herself, dead, inside

("Serenity is my favorite emotion," Barnabas
confesses to Sam over drinks at The Blue Whale,

after quitting tonight's portrait-sitting early).

———————————————————

Those things in that room in the basement—
the locked room—don't mention them

again, Carolyn. Don't trust a doctor
who says, "I've taken some blood tests

and I'll run tests on them to see
what the corpuscles are up to."

Maggie wanders off into the graveyard
on Eagle Hill the way the elderly

walk away from nursing homes
and stumble into traffic.

The episode impossible to fit into
one sentence: howling dogs getting closer

and the doctor asks Maggie if she stuck
a pin in her neck right before he begins

the only blood-transfusion house call
in the history of American soap opera.

Maybe Maggie's just a sleepwalker.

———————————————

Victoria tells it the only way she knows,
another dark and tragic introduction:

"out of the tempestuous blackness
comes a horror that can't be explained"

(blame scriptwriter Malcolm Marmorstein,
who did 15 episodes of *Peyton Place*

the next year, 1968, and in 1993 wrote
and directed *Love Bites*, which starred

Adam Ant as vampire Zachary Simms).

———————————————

I understand, Maggie—I, too, expected
Barnabas would break into my bedroom

in the middle of the night. My jugular
was yours in close-up, moist bite marks

throbbing double-time. "That room
the nurse had left open just a crack,"

the doctor says, pointing to the window
where Maggie disappeared, "was wide open."

Poor Willie, everyone's sado-masochistic
toy, beaten by Barnabas with his wolf's-

head cane and, now, slapped bloody
by Jason, who claims, "I'm prepared

to go all the way, my boy."

———————————————

Wearing Josette's wedding dress—
the love of Barnabas's eighteenth-

century life—Maggie walks down
the staircase in time with the catatonic

music box in her left hand. Willie pretends
he's maître d': remembers to call Maggie

"Josette," adjusts the candlesticks
originally part of Josette's dowry

(bought in France, where a silversmith
made them from Josette's own design—

"You always had impeccable taste,"
Barnabas says, then asks her to play

that wretched music box again.)

———————————————

Roger, put down your third glass of sherry
and hire a psychic governess for your son—

Little David sitting next to Barnabas,
his clairvoyant antennae unable to detect

this is a dead man who sleeps all day
in a coffin. This must be how I spent

Memorial Day, 1967: watching Episode 241
with my mother (later, many nightmares

of Barnabas's reproving and predatory
glare at Little David). I agree, Burke,

it's not a skirmish between corpuscles;
when you examine a blood sample "under

a microphone," it's not mysterious at all.

———————————————

Watching an episode with Liz, Michael, Trish,
winter vacation in San Diego, the four of us

sharing weed-spiked Rice Krispies Treats
and chocolate covered almonds, unraveling

the mysterious Theremin in the *Dark Shadows*
theme music—"It's like the first synthesizer,"

Michael says, imitating the instrument's
science-fiction whistle; "it's in the Beach Boys,

'Good Vibrations,' and Radiohead uses it, too."
I promised them Mrs. Stoddard would botch

her lines, but her performance was flawless
(tonight, though, she blundered again,

an episode I saw alone, back in Chicago).

———————————————

"I guess some of the most beautiful sights
I've ever seen have been microscopic views

of hideous malignancies," says Dr. Woodard,
who nevertheless is terrified of Maggie's blood.

An entire episode without a vampire—
at least I got to see Roger toss back

two more glasses of sherry. Signs that Sam
is an artist: rolls up only one of his shirt sleeves,

smokes a pipe whose bowl is carved to look
like Ben Franklin, forgets to eat, paints

a vampire in the middle of the night,

can't control his temper, paces his studio

with brush in hand (and he's a purist—
Burke invites Sam to dinner and promises,

"We can knock your pet hate, pop art").

——————————————————

David (Trinidad, not Little David, the psychic
child), sent an Amazon link this morning

for *Dark Shadows: The Complete Original Series*,
1,225 episodes (I will compose one sentence

for each), priced $539.99—he's written
300 *Peyton Place* haiku over three years,

understands I'll find a way to afford it—
and I noticed a customer review anticipating

a "soon-to-be-released" *Dark Shadows* film
starring Johnny Depp (who would require

several coats of Barnabas's eye shadow just
to resemble a vampire); I worried all day

the film could rob my poem of relevance,
as if I'm writing star-fuck verse instead

of excavating childhood night terrors,
though I really tried to feel gratitude

for Depp: as David reminded me,
Dark Shadows: The Complete Original Series

exists only because of the new movie,
as a promo vehicle—in a coffin-shaped

DVD box I want, badly, to own, even if
the medium is obsolete by the time I write

this poem's 1,225th and final sentence—
and after pre-ordering the complete series

tonight, I witnessed the most terrifying
episode thus far: down went the coffin lid

on screaming Maggie, the scene shot
first-person POV, an utterly psychotic way

for director Lela Swift to tell this story
(what compelled Swift, who also

directed the first and last episodes
of *Dark Shadows*, to decide that all of us

watching on 6/7/67, especially my mother
and me, her toddler son, should feel

as if Barnabas just buried us alive?).

———————————————

There's something about that room
in the basement: keeping it under

lock and key for 18 years is bound
to invite a certain amount of curiosity—

especially for those of us who can't shake
the image from our heads of Maggie

buried alive for a night in the Collins tomb.
It's taken 40 episodes to hear the echo

of my mother's name, "Margaret," in Maggie,
who sits at the Victorian gothic mirror

in her bedroom prison, locked inside
by Barnabas, and tries fitfully to remember

who she is—"Maggie, yes, Maggie, that's
your name," she says, "that's *my* name,

I must remember that, 'Maggie' for 'Margaret,'
I am Maggie Evans"—the night after I dream

my mother, Margaret, now 10 years dead,
appeared in the kitchen of an abandoned

house where I squatted in Chicago's
Logan Square neighborhood, wanted

to hear about my new writing projects
as I made her a grilled cheese sandwich;

and if she were alive tonight, I'd ask:
back in 1967, when we watched this episode

together (10 days before my first birthday),
was she angry like I am now, in my living room,

that Maggie opened her shameless music box
once more and inflicted its merry-go-round

melody on us, over and over and over.

2.

A darkness of the spirit, a darkness of the mind, a darkness of the will: the foundations of Collinwood lie deep in the age-old rock.

I can't be sure if Barnabas is a sadist
or surrealist: "Perhaps you'll come

to find madness is preferable to sanity,"
he says, flashing silent-movie bug eyes

at Maggie (now locked in his basement
dungeon), "or death preferable to life."

Suddenly, Carolyn is queen of a motorcycle
gang, raising a toast to more horsepower

and louder exhaust with new boyfriend,
Buzz, at the Blue Whale. I wish Victoria's

introductions for each episode could be
Joy Division songs: "The wind from the sea

announces that soon no light will shine
at all / but the dark that lies ahead is not

the deepest dark to be found this night."
—————————————————

What a thrill: at a Logan Square party for
Bernadette Mayer, the night after Jason

coerces Mrs. Stoddard into setting a date
for their wedding and Carolyn announces

she's marrying Buzz after a two-episode
courtship, Bernadette read my favorites,

"Carlton Fisk" and "X on Page 50 at half-
inch intervals"; and Lisa Janssen told me

she, too, watched *Dark Shadows* as a child
with her mother—she used to read about

Barnabas in *Teen Beat*—and earlier that day
she saw the trailer for Johnny Depp's new film

and was appalled ("A bunch of easy jokes

about the 1970s," she said, "and Johnny Depp

washed out in ghoulish makeup—think about it,
can you remember the last time Tim Burton

made a good film?"). I had seen the trailer
myself that same morning, from a link sent

by Jan Bottiglieri, who warned, "Maybe it's best
to learn from those who care about us than

'on the street'; if you haven't seen this trailer,
prepare yourself, and I'm sorry," and I took

a breath and watched the three-minute preview
and couldn't believe how terrible it actually was:

Depp plays Barnabas slapstick—not the sociopath
of my childhood nightmares, instead a goofball

in clownish white-face plopped in the wrong
century for the sake of pratfalls and gags

and adolescent jokes about Eva Green's breasts;
in short, nothing like Barnabas now, tonight,

so touched by his own cruelty he trips over
his lines, lying to Maggie that her father stopped

the search for her and thinks she's dead
(don't worry, Maggie, a ghost girl will appear

outside your basement dungeon cell before
the credits roll and keep you company

singing "London Bridge Is Falling Down").

———————————————

Episode 256: I turned one year old the day
my mother and I watched Maggie's ghost girl,

dressed in eighteenth-century bonnet and lace,
toss a ball up and down 82 times (then another

seven playing catch with Little David, the psychic
child, who, in two different scenes, pretends he's

a kangaroo in Collinwood, hopping around
the estate in mop-top and demented smile).

My first-birthday hangover: did I really spend
an hour staring at a freeze-frame closeup of Buzz,

trying to make him look like Lenny Bruce?
Did the camera really just bump, mid-zoom,

into Maggie's cell door, or should I believe
Collinsport suffered a minor earthquake?

"Who would've guessed that Mrs. Stoddard,
who murdered her husband 18 years ago

and buried him in the basement, is agoraphobic?"
I said to Liz, who always seems to catch episodes

with me in which Barnabas doesn't appear.

————————————————

Listen—through a grate in Maggie's dungeon
wall, the Song of the Wandering Ghost Girl:

"One, two, away they flew; three, four,
by the door; five, six, count the bricks;

seven, eight, the clue is grate; nine, ten—
home again." Sam stumbles on Maggie half-

dead and limp on the gnarled beach below
Widows' Hill, as prophesied by Ghost Girl

in her impossible Cockney/Baltimore *patois*.
Today the part of Burke Devlin will be played

by Anthony George, replacing Mitch Ryan,
who will tell *TV Guide*: "I was so drunk that

year, I barely remember what *Dark Shadows*
was about." Joe, square-jawed, too articulate

and eager, munching a sandwich at the dock
in his windbreaker: Carolyn is falling for a guy

who looks like he beats up hippies—not that
anyone in Collinsport actually has an opinion

on the war (the Viet Cong aren't nearly scary
as a 207-year-old, blood-drinking dead man

with wolf's-head cane who locked a woman
in a prison cell below his mansion because

she refused to be his vampire-wife).

————————————————

Jason, glam-rock smoking jacket sashed
over his suit, pours Roger a glass of sherry

(of course) in the Great House drawing room
and, later, Barnabas offers Roger a draught

of Amontillado (shades of Poe—fool's bells
jingling!) in the Old House. Dr. Hoffman

is less likely to say Sam can't see Maggie if he's
already there: this koan will agitate my mind

tomorrow during morning meditation.
This was a day to write about in my diary,

seeing the inside of Mrs. Stoddard's bedroom
for the first time (as the Three Widows, ghosts

for whom the cliff is named, keen for her
to leap from Widows' Hill onto stock-footage

rocks below), and when I came to work I found
Dark Shadows: The Complete Original Series

sitting in my office—a coffin within a packing

box within another packing box (131 discs,

1,225 episodes for 470 hours, limited edition
number 369 of 2,000, and a collector's postcard

autographed in silver ink by Jonathan Frid,
Barnabas himself)—as promised, I took

a cell photo of the complicated UPS package
for my bandmate, Brian, who warned me after

rehearsal last week about advertisements plastered
on buses for the film and a huge Johnny Depp

billboard staring down on traffic in Wicker Park;
I needed both hands and a steady back to heft

the coffin into a cab after my night class.

_____

I planned a break from the poem tonight,
but news flashed that Jonathan Frid died,

the day after my limited-edition coffin arrived,
and in this moment, not quite sure how I

feel about outliving the star of my childhood
nightmares—scared I wrote "outliving," fear I'm

smugly tempting the universe to hasten my
own demise (this is my poem, but it's Frid's life,

after all)—I decided to watch the Fourth of July
1967 episode: after Barnabas sneaks up behind

Mrs. Stoddard and grabs her, stopping a suicide
leap off Widows' Hill, the vampire confides,

"Death is fascinating when one considers the wide
possibilities it offers," confirming for me tonight,

April 19, 2012, my homage is to watch and rhyme.

_____

Making a peanut butter sandwich the night
before Roger appears in a scene where nobody

actually reaches for a bottle, I did the math:
470 hours means 20 full days of my life

watching *Dark Shadows* for this poem
(then I remembered explaining to my

sixth-grade teacher the first epic obsession,
why I collected cash register sales slips

not coins, or stamps, or baseball cards).

———————————————

Another night of Sesame Street jazz,
mashed-up surf guitar and ersatz bebop,

at the Blue Whale. "Mad? Who's mad?"
Carolyn shouts to Joe after the Tito Puente

mambo knockoff on the jukebox finally
ends—"Unless you mean 'crazy' mad . . .

I think that's where I'll go on my
honeymoon . . . I think I'll go crazy!"

Mrs. Stoddard interrupts her own wedding
to confess she killed her first husband—

the fourth straight episode I've seen without
Barnabas since Jonathan Frid died—

a scene so important ABC repeated it
two consecutive episodes. "I'm going

to have to do some digging in the basement,"
Sheriff Patterson says; I feel the same about

my psyche every time Barnabas appears
on screen and nightmares like this one

come back: his silhouette, with cane,
cast by street lamp against my bedroom

window—hungry vampire waiting for little
boy to fall asleep (and now five episodes

I've seen with no Barnabas since Frid died).
————————————————

"Why have I had these nightmares
night after night after night?" says

Mrs. Stoddard, shaking in her polka-dot
wedding Mumu after Sheriff Patterson

reveals the trunk exhumed from her
basement is empty—no husband's

corpse, and no Barnabas in the six
episodes I've seen since Frid died.

Barnabas returns after his six-episode
vacation and, trembling over a string

of pearls from Josette's jewelry box,
flubs a particularly evil soliloquy:

"Nothing can be bought . . . but the next
'Josette' . . . I have in mind . . . not even

with the entire contents of this chest . . .
perhaps that's why I'm so attracted to her."

Jason slaps Willie around again (it's feeling
more like a courtship ritual than a fight

between thugs); "I'm not leaving until
I get what I came for," Jason says,

and he gets it, all right—Barnabas's hand
rising from the coffin as Jason lifts its lid,

vampire fingers gripping the grave-robber's

Adam's apple, recalling Episode 210,

first sentence of this poem, when Willie
busted Barnabas from the Collins tomb

and the vampire found his way to Collinwood
posing as a long-lost British cousin with

impeccable courtly manners who coincidentally
looked exactly like the portrait of his namesake

(the resemblance was uncanny, everyone said,
and even Little David, the psychic child,

was fooled) hanging in the Great House parlor:
I barely had language yet, all memories at this age

almost primeval, just wordless shapes and colors,
sensations and nightmares, but I remember

being terrified by Barnabas's immediate adaptation
to the modern world, straight from the grave

to 1967, dead nearly two centuries and now
just another aristocrat in Vietnam-era Maine,

which couldn't be more different than Johnny
Depp's Barnabas from the film, which I saw today

with Liz and Brian—a slapstick, fish-out-of-water
vampire bewildered by McDonald's arches,

paved roads, automobiles, movie theaters,
telephones, traffic lights, the Milton Bradley

board game Operation, miniskirts,
photographs, macramé, backhoes,

waffles, electric pianos, Karen Carpenter,
televisions, psychiatry, and lava lamps

(Liz: "Johnny Depp made Barnabas look
like Willie Wonka"; Brian: "It was better

than *The Avengers*, which isn't saying much.")

————————————————

"Isn't it supposed to be scary?" Megan Draper
asked in this week's episode of *Mad Men*,

preparing her friend Julia for a *Dark Shadows*
audition (oh, god, this means Ghost Girl—

revealed tonight as Barnabas's sister who died
in 1796, when she was 10—might haunt a future

Mad Men episode, playing catch with herself
and singing "London Bridge Is Falling Down"

in a corner of Roger Sterling's mod, Op Art
office). I can't believe Barnabas, on the balcony

with Vicki, thinks his melancholic vampire-talk
is flirting: "But see how beautiful the moon is—

when one considers the moon takes on its
beauty reflecting the rays of the sun, it seems

inconceivable the sun could be so ugly."
How could an exquisite and entertaining

evening possibly harm Vicki, except that
it's a costume party and she's been asked

by Barnabas to come as his dead Josette.

————————————————

As I watched the episode from my mother's 41st
Birthday (aired 7/20/67), I looked for personal

Clues that would summon her, guessing which
Dark Shadows characters she identified with

(Essentially, any of the witchy ones) and tried to
Figure out why, despite my nightmares, she

Gave up and let me watch the show with
Her—though the answer is probably simple:

I threw tantrums so I wouldn't miss Barnabas's
Josette fixations, starting with the night he

Kidnapped Maggie; there's my answer, I guess:
Logically, my mother, Margaret, identified with

Maggie, her namesake; and I know, recalling my
Nightmares, my shoulders hunched at bedtime,

Obviously I suffered with Maggie and Vicki
(Probably the first time I saw myself in a woman)

—Quite a stretch that an insomniacal one-year old could
Remember all this detail before coming into language,

So I'll just mark my mother's 41st birthday episode
Transcribing another epic Barnabas flub: I don't

Understand why, after ABC gave him a six-episode
Vacation, he couldn't stop himself from saying to

Willie, "That night must go nothing wrong"
(Exactly, Barnabas, and it's not a good omen

You just uttered this sentence backwards).

———————————————

Zero patience for the costume ball:
if Barnabas knew how to flirt, he might

not have to woo Vicki with such an
elaborate ruse—a party where everyone

in the family comes dressed as an
eighteenth-century Collins ancestor

and drinks claret cups ladled from
an antique punch bowl by a vampire

whose father (or, more accurately,

a man, Roger, dressed as his father)

keeps insisting they all perform a séance.
Now that the ghosts and eighteenth-

century period costumes have completely
blurred past, present, and future, making

Dark Shadows even more complicated
to write about—Josette takes over Vicki's

body and speaks through her, re-experiencing
her death 172 years ago, but present-day

Barnabas (from 1967) breaks the circle
at the séance table to prevent Josette's

spirit from revealing the vampire himself
chased her off the cliff at Widows' Hill

that night in 1795—I worry I'm not writing
a long poem but building an impossible object

like Ken Applegate's "Matchstick Space Shuttle,"
which I saw this weekend at the Ripley's

Believe It or Not! Museum's Odditorium
in San Francisco (later, roaming the museum's

mirror maze in 3-D glasses, I envied Applegate's
persistence: 10 years to design his shuttle—

with round, retractable wheels and functional
wing flaps—then 12 years and 10,000 hours

to build it with a million wooden matchsticks).

————————————————

In psychotherapy with Dr. Hoffman,
Maggie presses her fingertips against

her temples to block memories of Barnabas's
horrific tinkling music box; I've tried this

myself, Maggie, and it's no use—the show's
writers keep inserting it into the plot, anyway.

Dr. Hoffman takes her back to the cemetery
on Eagle Hill, where Josette's gravestone,

hidden by a clump of elm trees, reads,
"Born 1800 / Died 1822," which makes

no sense because Barnabas fell in love
with Josette in the early 1790s, before

he became a vampire; maybe I should heed
Burke's advice to Vicki when she claims

to see Maggie walking in the graveyard:
"It was an imagination—you saw something

you really didn't see," (is it "an imagination"
that Anthony George, the new actor playing Burke,

is a dead ringer for pre-Guyana Jim Jones—
that Vicki is unlucky enough to be courted

simultaneously by a vampire who can't flirt
and a religious demagogue who will massacre

908 acolytes in the jungle 11 years from now?).
"Nothing that happens on earth can be termed

'unearthly,'" Dr. Hoffman says, clenching her
sadistic mouth as she prepares to infiltrate

Collinwood disguised as a family genealogist.

———————————————————————

Sometimes all I want to do is transcribe
Vicki's grim, overwrought introductions

to each episode: "The sea is never still;
the unseen moon beckons the massive

watery waste, and almost against its will
the sea is drawn from the shore in tidal

obedience to a distant force"—long pause,
heaven help me, Vicki, please don't stop—

"and so, sometimes, it is with us."

———————————————

Hunch your shoulders, Vicki, before you
fall asleep in Josette's bed—it's how I

survived my own nights of close proximity
to Barnabas. "What a classic soap opera shot,

talking to each other's backs while they're
facing the camera," Liz says, watching Vicki

in front of Mrs. Stoddard in front of
Dr. Hoffman, the three women framed

like dominoes; double-bonus for her: Barnabas
actually appears in this episode—fangs poised

over Vicki's bulging jugular—and a live
microphone picks up a stagehand coughing

off-camera on the set of Barnabas's parlor.
Little David, the psychic child, gets a funny

feeling Vicki is somebody else, while of course
he walks around Collinwood thinking Barnabas

is just another prim, anachronistic uncle who
only comes out at night (and whose reflection

can't be seen in Dr. Hoffman's compact mirror).

———————————————

Now it's clear: the cloying tune of Josette's
music box is nothing but a common ice-cream-

truck melody, like the one that passed through my

neighborhood summer nights when I was a boy;

"I especially love the tinkling sound it makes,"
says Vicki, lolling and glazed since the séance.

Which is more musical, John Cage asked,
a truck passing by a factory or a truck

passing by a music school—Vicki's fluttering
inflections when she asks Barnabas to take back

the music box, or the two of them trying to talk
over another off-camera cough caught by live

microphone while a fire extinguisher goes off
("Until I die there will be sounds," Cage said,

"and they will continue following my death").

3.

*There is the feeling at Collinwood that time has been
suspended. Danger is everywhere, at all times.
Even the dead can still be dangerous.*

As if she senses this poem's entire structure
is temporarily askew, Dr. Hoffman, the first

person to open Barnabas's coffin without
losing her life (or her mind), sounds out each

word like an overwhelmed second-grader as
she (not Vicki) introduces episode 291,

first one I've watched on a disc from
the DVD coffin—and I should confess

now, as Section 3 begins, the limited-
edition casket has forced me to revise

the poem's original structural plan:
after opening the coffin two months ago,

the day before Jonathan Frid died,
I realized the length of each section

must be extended from 40 sentences
(corresponding to the 40 episodes

in each of the two boxes of discs I
bought on Amazon prior to the coffin's

arrival) to 55 sentences (the number of
episodes in each DVD box in the coffin);

and, to further complicate my grandiose
mathematical ambitions, this poem actually

doesn't open with Episode 1 of *Dark Shadows*,
but with number 210, when Willie busts

Barnabas from the Collins family tomb
and the vampire descends on Collinsport,

because, for me, and for most *Dark Shadows*
viewers, the soap opera didn't really begin

until Barnabas rose from the grave (though

I've planned an Appendix with a sentence

for each pre-Barnabas episode); in short,
my structure was fucked the moment

I opened the DVD coffin and discovered
this poem's master plan must be rearranged

to account for the new 55-episode boxes,
which is why Section 3, the first to work

with the limited-edition discs, might not be
as long as the others—it's a transition

between the old 40-episode DVD boxes
and the 55-episode boxes in the coffin;

my god, all this talk about the number
of sentences per section feels like I'm

obsessing over the number of wooden
matchsticks required for an impossible

object, this 1,225-episode Space Shuttle,
when I should be paying attention

to Dr. Woodard, who takes off his
thick black glasses after delivering twins

and looks like Robert Lowell staring off
a ledge, which is pretty much how Willie

experiences every day of his life serving
Barnabas (though now Willie claims

he can live without feeling something
terrible will happen any minute)—

and, as I imagine the author of *Life Studies*
actually is a doctor studying the undead,

a fly lands above Barnabas's left eye in tight
close-up, then a few seconds later buzzes

his face and Barnabas swats him away
with the same autocratic panache he brought

to the recurring nightmare where he felt
around the rim of my bedroom window

for weak points of entry (eventually, in later
dream incarnations, he abandoned pretense

and simply broke the window with his cane).

————————————————

I'm watching *Dark Shadows* in Paris,
in Manal and Tal's Belleville apartment,

rain falling on the glass roof of their
office as Liz and Tal collaborate on

a paper for a post-colonialism conference
and Dr. Hoffman claims, like a soap-opera

Faustus, that medicine is about to break
the barrier between life and death—

Liz and I could've used a dose of Dr. Hoffman's
medicine earlier this afternoon, looking for

Apollinaire's grave at Pére Lachaise, where,
each time I consulted our graveyard map,

we found ourselves intruding on grieving
families as we tried (and failed) to find

the *ici repose* resting place of the famous
surrealist, forgetting this was still a cemetery,

a sacred place, an esteemed ancient maze
of graves in Paris where people mourn

their loved ones, not a tourist walk
in Hollywood, the two of us lost

and shambling among the mossy
chestnut trees of Pére Lachaise—

we could feel them growing, bushes
and branches upstarting beneath

the tombs—with a map of grave plots,
not a guide to movie stars' homes,

soggy from the downpour; if only
we could've summoned Ghost Girl,

who tells Little David, the psychic child,
"You know about leaves and everything,

and, well, I know who's dead and who isn't."

––––––––––––––––––––––––––

Barnabas reminds Willie he's a bottom,
bred to serve him eternally and take it

like a man—the vampire nervous in
the candlelight gauze of his parlor,

preparing to leave for the abandoned
House by the Sea, where he and Burke

and Jim Jones will compete like schoolboys
to impress Vicki. Sounds like Procol Harum

on the Blue Whale jukebox tonight,
no coincidence "A Whiter Shade of Pale"

reached #10 on Billboard the same week
this episode was filmed (#1 on the U.K.

singles chart all summer): a scotch and
water for Vicki, bourbon for Burke,

and for Barnabas a bottle of Tru-Blood?
"Good news: this program, *Dark Shadows*,

is now being presented in color": I never

knew Vicki's dress is red, Burke's face

is riven with smoker's lines, Barnabas
needs so many layers of foundation

and eye shadow to look like a dead man,
Maggie's hair ribbon is yellow, the walls

of Dr. Woodard's office are, like my scooter,
seafoam green (his lampshades burgundy),

and Dr. Hoffman's jacket is royal blue.
We are in Oz now, *Dark Shadows* in color

Every episode; Liz persuaded me to watch
Another one tonight—"It looks like a

Real soap opera now, in color"—but it's
Episode 296, the color videotape master

Irretrievably lost (ABC's careless archiving),
Nothing but a black-and-white kinescope copy

Of washed-out images, murky close-ups; our
Zeal to catch another episode in Paris

Now reduced to dull grays, scratchy video,
Off-white candle flames, distorted soundtrack

Warbling from my laptop's tiny speakers.

————————————————

Bit by spiders in the Paris studio we rented,
by flies at Lake Michigan the day after

we returned to the States, stung by a bee
the Fourth of July at David Trinidad's—

where he gave me as a birthday gift
Dario Argento's 1977 film *Suspiria*

("Happy Belated Birthday! I expect to see
this mentioned in *Dark Shadows*—don't you

love a present with strings attached!"),
first film of Argento's "Three Mothers"

trilogy, starring Joan Bennett (Mrs. Stoddard
of *Dark Shadows*) as Madam Blanc, owner

of a supernatural European dance company
—bites on my arms and legs, swollen stinger

wound throbbing my neck, I attract blood-
suckers and biters now that I'm immersed

in the show's abrupt shift to color videotape:
Joe, in olive drab pencil pants and forest green

sweater—ROTC chic, I actually prefer it
to the cluttered black-and-green afghan

slung over Sam's antique, marbled sofa—
in color *Dark Shadows* loses some goth,

but Sam's eyes don't look like Rasputin's
in black-and-white, and Barnabas's silhouette

outside Maggie's French doors feeds a little
boy's nightmares no matter what color

this scene happens to be filmed in.

————————————————

Carolyn posed in pastel green like
a mannequin in front of dappled

stained glass—she's getting an odd
feeling and doesn't know why.

"Imagine what it's like to exist only
at night, only when the world

is at peace," Barnabas, flirting, says
to Vicki, "it would be a lifetime of

moonlights" (ouch, an embarrassing
"I-fall-upon-the-thorns-of-life-I-bleed!"

moment from writer Ron Sproat,
the man who created Barnabas

for the show and recommended his
old friend Jonathan Frid for the role;

after his first on-set meeting with Frid,
Executive Producer and series creator

Dan Curtis was unimpressed: "That's
our vampire?" Curtis said, "Jesus—

he looks like Edward Everett Horton!").

————————————————

Another color videotape missing from
ABC's archive: Episode 300 murky

in monochromatic kinescope, Barnabas
behind a flickering candelabra in full-

Nosferatu glare, later the vampire breaks
eye-contact with the camera like a penitent

child, an expression that would've soothed
my nightmares had he stooped to express

such vulnerability in them; Dr. Hoffman
threatens to stop the blood treatments that

would cure his vampirism if Barnabas sneaks
into Vicki's bedroom again and opens

Josette's music box (stalker alert: Burke
proposes to Vicki and vows, "I'll ask you

tomorrow and the next day and the day
after that until you break down and say 'yes'")

—much emotional turbulence in Collinsport

the night I returned from a weekend with Liz,

David T., and Jeffery Conway
at Camp Chesterfield, the American

Spiritualist community founded in 1886,
where numerologist Patricia Kennedy

explained to us over lunch at Denny's,
"There's light, medium, and deep trances,

honey, and you better watch out for
deep because it'll knock you out:

one time I was in a deep trance
during a séance and when the lights

came back on, I looked down and saw
my teeth were on the floor: a woman

who heard her father's voice coming
out of me was skeptical because

it didn't really sound like him, but the last
three years of his life he didn't have teeth—

so Spirit knocked out my teeth as a way
of saying, 'Look, it's *that* guy talking'";

later, after a story about apporting a bouquet
of paranormal flowers out of nowhere

into a séance (and repeated advice
not to order Denny's seasoned fries),

Patricia, who once said I try so hard
to be an ethical person because in a past

life I was a religious charlatan who
bilked my disciples of all their money

(I entered this body, she told me, solely
to atone), now warned I'm spending

too much time in the spirit world, not
enough in the physical: well, what do you

expect—I've been hanging around
haunted Collinsport all summer with

a vampire, a psychic child, and a ghost girl.

————————————————————

Burke and Vicki kissing outside the doors
of Collinwood: must all *Dark Shadows*

smooching be so stiff and awkwardly feral?
"I'll be giving your injection in 20 minutes,"

Dr. Hoffman announces to Barnabas,
whose garish, black, pre-Raphaelite

smoking jacket only makes sense if
it's a side effect of the blood treatments.

Musclebound blunt and dumbfounded,
as usual, Joe doesn't see how the sound

of soft music could have anything to do
with the terrifying experience Maggie's

been through—obviously, the insipid
tinkle of Josette's music box triggers

no memories of ice-cream-truck melodies
from his childhood—and now I know

my relentless boredom as a boy might
have sprouted from the same place

as my night terrors, from identification
with Maggie, my mother's namesake,

doomed to hunch my shoulders
every night to protect my neck from

Barnabas's fangs and bored beyond
relief at daylight: "Pass the time of day,

then I pass the time of night," she says,
pacing the living room, trapped at home

by Joe and Sam, who fear the kidnapper
will snatch her again if she goes outside,

"then it's time to pass the time of day again."

———————————————————

There will be time to prepare a face to
meet, Maggie, the faces that you meet—

to give thanks you're not bored
as the bartender at the Blue Whale,

enduring those same two faux-surf
bebop tunes playing over and over

on the jukebox (but for Episode 294,
last one shot black-and-white, and

the song that sounded so much like
Procol Harum, "Whiter Shade of Pale").

Fourteenth anniversary of my move
from Boston to Chicago, and Ghost Girl

takes Little David, the psychic child,
to a secret place no one knows about—

"Hey, there's a coffin," Little David says,
voice rising to the same incredulous pitch

he uses when he talks to dead Josette.
Last night, my first Barnabas dream

since the early 1970s—I remember it
now, watching the shadow of a boom mic

crawl across the wall of the Great House

parlor: I was held prisoner by Barnabas,

whose nemesis, the witch Angelique
(she won't actually appear on the show

for another 62 episodes), snuck into my
cell and gave me a very important tip:

coffee will protect you from vampires.

————————————————————

"Pop, that's called whistling in the dark,"
Maggie says, and she doesn't mean the "dark"

from Vicki's latest emo-girl episode
intro: "It is a special kind of darkness

the night brings to Collinwood," she intones.
Sheriff Patterson is bumbling in the dark,

and Sam looks more and more like Rasputin
in these episodes shot in color videotape—dark

circles under his eyes the mark of an insomniac
who paints all night in jacket and tie, *Dark*

Shadows's moody artist making a plan to draw
a mysterious ghost girl out from the dark

(the key, Sam, is Little David, who's played
with her under the elm trees in the dark

Collins tomb on Eagle Hill—but he won't
talk until he's back from Bangor, after dark).

Barnabas clutches a rare book, Ghost Girl haunts
Dr. Hoffman: Collinwood comes alive after dark.

A coffin lid goes down on yet another character:
Little David, caught in the cemetery after dark,

hiding from Barnabas in an empty casket.

————————————————————

Close-up: Little David inside the coffin
breathing heavily, sealed inside the Collins

tomb in a secret room: a ten-year-old
trapped among the dead on daytime TV,

buried alive between *General Hospital*
and *The Dating Game*—how could

Little David's plight not give every kid
watching this episode a nightmare

(later, the psychic child shaking with
tears when he tries to pry open the door

of the secret room with his penknife);
I confess that rendering Little David's

primal terror distracts from my guilt
for not writing about my father

in the previous episode—he turned 46
the day it aired (my age now), and I can

re-create from memories of his rote habits
what he probably did that day: it was a Friday,

he woke before sunrise for calisthenics
in the living room, then toast and coffee

before riding his bicycle (a flashlight
in his basket to shine in the eyes of dogs

who might attack, blinding them long enough
to pedal away) three blocks to the factory

where he inspected steel all day for burrs
and other imperfections, home by five

for dinner (I'll assume my mother
made him a cake that particular day),

at some point finding his way to the couch,
exhausted, to read the afternoon newspaper,

sports page first, then op-eds, especially
his favorite columnist Ed Mathews,

whose homespun Garrison Keillor wit,
like a yokel squinting through the sunlight

while he chews a blade of grass, I would
come to detest by high school, when I

discovered Philip K. Dick—my best
friend Kurt passing me Dick's *VALIS*

in English class, and in the first passage
I randomly flipped to the narrator says,

"They ought to make it a binding clause
that if you find God you get to keep him"

—and my father fell asleep, snoring wickedly,
until the sound of the crinkling newspaper

slipping out of his hand awoke him.

————————————————————

Barnabas, half obscured by gloomy eye shadow,
blinks in the seven-branch candelabra shadows.

Predictable: the aging cemetery caretaker
is mad as a hatter, afraid of his own shadow.

Dr. Hoffman caught suppressing a sneeze
(they never shoot extra takes on *Dark Shadows*)

and Dr. Woodard consults an authority on toys,
Miss Spence, who's certain beyond the shadow

of a doubt Ghost Girl's doll is over 150 years old;
Willie hears "London Bridge" in the shadow

of this red rock—Ghost Girl playing the recorder:

she's sneaky and capricious, like Willie's shadow

at morning striding behind him in this waste
land of gnarled shrubbery, or like his shadow

at evening rising to meet him (is it wrong
I'm rereading Eliot while, in the shadows

of Eagle Hill, Little David rots in a sealed tomb?).
Sundown, the passing of Barnabas's shadow

across the screen, the twitch of Dr. Hoffman's
mouth: someone please say the word "shadow"

so I can finish the final line of my ghazal.

_____

Little David escapes(!)—then runs straight
into the arms of Barnabas, proving no child

is safe in Collinsport and no doubt spawning
nightmares for little boys watching this episode

("David, you're acting as though you're afraid
of me," Barnabas says, sticking out his wolf's-

head cane to block the psychic child from
running away—the same cane that broke

my bedroom window in nightmares—
then later, right before the credits roll,

Barnabas's parting words, a hypnotic message
sent psychically across the Collinwood estate

to Little David who, like me as a child,
is struck with insomnia because of a vampire:

"Good night, David—pleasant dreams,"
Barnabas says, in cruel, sarcastic voiceover);

after following his mausoleum plight
so closely for six episodes, I couldn't

resist looking up Little David on Wikipedia
to see what became of actor David Henesy,

fearing yet another sad tale of a child star
who grows up to be a shoplifter or an addict

(though can he really be called a "star"
when he forgets his lines so much),

then got distracted and looked up Joe instead—
too-articulate paragon of bourgeois Collinsport

who looks like the high school football star
and student council president who volunteers

for Vietnam after graduation—and I discovered
actor Joel Crothers died of AIDS in 1985,

two years before AZT, and he was
only 44, not much younger than another

Joe, we called him Joe-Joe, my favorite
uncle, who contracted HIV in Los Angeles

and moved back to Erie, Pennsylvania,
to die in 1991, surrounded mostly by

mean-spirited Italians who could not
bring themselves to utter the word "gay"

—I say "mostly" because I remember
my mother spent every day with him

in the hospital at the end (though she told
anyone outside the family tribe it was cancer)

and took care of Joe-Joe, her little brother
born deaf and mute, like she did when

she was a teenager and the rest of the family,
in that awful immigrant paranoia of the time

(World War II, and half the neighborhood
supported Mussolini until the U.S. declared

war on Italy), treated the little boy's inability
to hear or speak as an embarrassing aberration,

a shame to the clan; my mother, who once
asked me to write a poem about the night

Joe-Joe broke from a deep coma and sat up
straight and stared at the hospital ceiling

like he'd tear it up, burn the fucker down:
it was always silent with Joe-Joe, in a family

that never learned to sign, but he raised
his arms and spoke (first time anyone ever

heard words come out of his mouth):
"When?" he asked over and over,

then smiled and lay back down to die.

————————————————————

Dr. Woodard vows to Sam they will
"examine that mausoleum from top

to bottom": it's skunk hour in Collinwood,
Robert Lowell and Rasputin poking around

the graveyard (scene shot in chroma key,
both men emanating eerie analog auras

against a gigantic stock photograph
of rows of headstones—obviously

fake background, like Halloween décor,
as the two make their trek to the Collins

mausoleum, clearing a path through
artificial soundstage foliage) on my first

full day in Middelburg, a thousand-year-old

town in The Netherlands, where I'm giving

a conference presentation on the collection
of Elise Cowen's poems I'm editing (mailed

a draft of the book manuscript to publisher
Janet Holmes four days before my flight):

I've landed in a sleepy gingerbread town
where 85 percent of the population owns

a bicycle—a beautiful sight, all these bikes,
for someone who lives in Chicago, where I

once counted seven SUVs lined up at a stoplight,
one behind the other, like a conga line of three-

hundred-pound football linemen; on the train
from Amsterdam to Middleburg yesterday,

I swore I saw an ostrich in a field of cows
and lambs—hallucination, of course,

jet-lagged from my overnight flight
through seven time zones and speeding

across verdant grasslands in the Dutch
countryside, a vision made stranger

that afternoon, when the restless whistling
of a parrot who lives in a seven-foot-tall

cage in the hotel bar woke me from a nap.

———————————————

Like a stubborn ballerina, Dr. Hoffman,
pursing her sadistic mouth, walks out

of the Great House into a thunderstorm.
"You're trying to make me afraid of my

own shadow," Maggie says to Sam
—why couldn't she say "shadow"

when I was writing the ghazal—
and everyone studiously avoids

eye contact with Sam's awful new
painting, half-finished, a morbid

swordfish prone on a boat deck.
Vicki's frothing introductions to each

episode are tolerable when I can pretend
she's describing my childhood, hunted

by Barnabas: "A frightened and disturbed
boy lies sleeping," she says, nearly panting,

as Little David twists his body back
and forth beneath the sheets—

nightmare of Barnabas on the prowl,
baring his fangs at the psychic child—

"but sleep brings him no peace, for dreams
can bring him one step closer to learning

a terrifying and dangerous secret."

———————————————

Barnabas talks through a stuffy nose.
Barnabas argues with his own voiceover.

Barnabas paces in psychedelic smoking jacket.
Barnabas's portrait gives Little David a nightmare.

Barnabas hears the psychic child's secret thoughts.
"Barnabas isn't dead *all* the time," Little David says.

Barnabas lurks in Little David's crystal ball.
Barnabas is afraid this will threaten his career.

Barnabas paces in dark overcoat and cape.
Barnabas wanted me dead, too, Little David—

Barnabas pallid and scheming at the window,
Barnabas rolling up his sleeve after an injection,

Barnabas's eyes in the portrait glowing;
Barnabas turns into a bat (a prop on a string,

prerecorded chirping) and torments Little David.

4.

*No night at Collinwood has ever been longer than
the one that is now almost over.*

Libraries shouldn't be so emotional:
I sat with my laptop at a long oak table

in the University of New Hampshire
archives, doing poem-research

in Betty Hill's papers—the world's
most famous UFO abductees,

Betty and Barney Hill, allegedly taken
aboard a spacecraft 51 years ago

in the White Mountains, about 100 miles
from my hotel—and my hands shook,

reading Betty's journal entry from
the day Barney was killed by a stroke:

after a game of pool in their basement,
the entire state shut down by a monster

February blizzard and Barney winning
every game, joking he could beat her with

one hand tied behind his back,
he felt a sting, like a hornet's,

in back of his neck and he collapsed;
ambulance delayed by unplowed roads,

he slipped into a coma less than
a half hour after finally making it

to the emergency room, the doctor telling
Betty it's hopeless, just pray he dies quickly;

that night, she wrote in her journal:
"I sat, wrapped in a blanket—

I thought it should have been a bearskin,
my living room should have been a cave

with a candle and fire hearth, while I
waited for 46-year-old Barney to die";

I looked around the archive, the Head
of Special Collections talking on the phone

about the library's Robert Frost Papers,
and three tables behind me a journalist

researched the Hills for a *Skeptical Inquirer*
article, taking digital photos of Betty's

correspondence—I don't think I've ever
felt such physical loss in the quiet,

walled-off vault of a library reading
room, taking notes from Betty's

words on a yellowing page composed
40 years ago (I forgot electric typewriters

allowed for a cursive font, her preferred
typeface for nearly everything she wrote);

I could hear in Betty's voice a grieving
monotone, eviscerated, the same exhausted

pitch I remember from my father
describing my mother's stroke in 1999:

she wrote a check to Mellon Bank
for their monthly car payment,

she was watching a *Matlock* repeat
and he heard a moan—an animal

heave, a keening, her body shrunk
into itself—and he found her moving

her mouth up and down, no sound,
eyes astonished and terrified, blood

crossing into her brain, destroying it;

I'm starting Section 4 of the poem with

too much death, I realized later in my
hotel room, when the DVD menu

listed the air date for tonight's episode:
October 2, 1967, the date of my brother's

10th birthday—and I'd watch it tonight,
10/2/12, six years after his death from

heart disease (coincidence, arriving
at the 10/2/67 episode on 10/2/12,

as if reading about aliens traveling
hundreds of light years wasn't enough

to imagine time is circular rather than linear,
that all moments in time exist at the same time);

but I didn't intend to start Section 4
with elegies, and Dr. Hoffman is subbing

for Vicki in tonight's über-goth episode
intro: "One boy"—Little David, attacked

by a rubber bat prop—"will live through
an experience so terrifying that his mind

will reel and for an instant his heart will
stop beating" . . . but his heart never

actually stops in this episode, not once,
and he falls fast asleep after Dr. Woodard

gives him a sedative (later awakened
by Ghost Girl cast in eerie blue light);

poor David Henesy had to roll
on the floor and scream for help

in the opening scene, pretend to be
terrorized by a rubber bat tied to a rod

held by a stagehand (and mistakenly
visible in shadow against the wall

of his character's bedroom), then cry,
"Cousin Barnabas hates me—he sent

the bat because he wants me to die."

———————————————————

Burke Devlin and Dr. Woodard stand
in the background, a pair of dour mimes

frowning in tandem. "You didn't
see the coffin," Little David says,

"and you didn't see the look on Barnabas's
face." The psychic child's inauspicious

introduction to his new psychiatrist:
here's the boy's crystal ball, which he

uses to find the ghost of a girl who
died in 1795 and plays with him

in the family tomb (note to shrink:
start therapy right away with Freud's

"The Theme of the Three Caskets").
"I'm not going to rest until I find out

why Sarah Collins has come back
to Earth," says Dr. Woodard, now

played by Peter Turgeon, after
Robert Gerringer fired for supporting

the September 22-October 3, 1967
National Association of Broadcast

Employees and Technicians strike:
Gerringer gone the episode before

his character encounters Ghost Girl
for the first time—tripping over

her lines, searching for the teleprompter
—among the three caskets of the Collins

mausoleum; Dr. Hoffman scoffs
when she's reminded that Maggie's

father, Sam, once met Ghost Girl, too:
"Sam Evans saw nothing: he's an artist,

a highly suggestible human being."
_____

Thanks to writer Gordon Russell,
this plot twist: hyperrational

skeptic Dr. Woodard (played by
Peter Turgeon, who resembles

a harried tax accountant—no
more Robert Lowell sightings for

me) is the only character
who believes Little David's claims

that dead people are coming back
to life in sleepy Collinsport.

This time, the vampire doesn't
forget his lines when he's trying

to bully the town physician.
The camera has a migraine—

erratic moves, blurs, streaks of blue,
whiplash close-up (Barnabas's

throat) followed by a curlicue
swirl into Dr. Hoffman's pout—

then the Collins family maid,

Mrs. Johnson, gets her first scene

in seventy-three episodes
and she promptly misses her cue.

Friday the 13th episode,
Dr. Hoffman describes a drug

she'll inject in Dr. Woodard
(who discovered Barnabas's

secret tonight) to make it ap-
pear he died of a heart attack—

what's next, Dr. Hoffman, cigars
for Castro coated in botu-

linum toxin, a ballpoint pen
loaded with a hypodermic

needle of insecticide, an
umbrella that can shoot pellets

of ricin, a wetsuit—Castro
again—contaminated with

bacteria that causes tu-
berculosis ("Murder is such

an ugly word," Barnabas says,
eight syllables in the line, "con-

sider it a mercy killing").

————————————————

A day of cold autumn rain, soggy
leaves, winter soon in Chicago,

and the rubber bat returns, a shabby
little prop fluttering outside doomed

Dr. Woodard's office window;
"The good doctor had a fatal curiosity,"

Barnabas says, after injecting Woodard
with Dr. Hoffman's heart-attack potion,

"now he doesn't have it anymore"
(no shortage of profundity in writer

Joe Caldwell's script: "A little knowledge
is a dangerous thing," Barnabas says earlier

in the episode, waving the hypodermic
in front of Dr. Woodard's face, "but a lot

of knowledge is even more dangerous").

——————————————————

I've always thought life in small-town
Maine was a little unhinged: Maggie

and Sam huddle below one of his
portraits, and I can't tell whether

it's a painting of Norman Mailer or
just a sad clown, and Sheriff Patterson,

played inexplicably by Angus Cairns
for the past two episodes, struts

around dead Dr. Woodard's office
like a yokel wannabe-academic:

"There is nothing supernatural about
Willie Loomis," Professor Patterson says,

"sub-natural would come closer to it."

——————————————————

What made Joe Caldwell decide the most
important object in Dr. Hoffman's

laboratory, amid her trellis of gurgling
beakers and tangled rubber tubes

("This magnificent structure," Barnabas
coos), should be a witch's cauldron.

Burke Devlin's plane crashes after
taking off from Belo Horizonte, Brazil—

his death foretold by Little David,
the psychic child, the same day I read

in Tim Reiterman's *Raven: The Untold
Story of the Rev. Jim Jones and His People*

that Jones traveled to Belo Horizonte
in 1963 because *Esquire* magazine named

it one of the 10 safest locations to survive
a nuclear war and rebuild civilization

(11 years later, Jones leased the land
that would become Jonestown, Guyana):

is it prophecy or merely narrative
foreshadowing that Anthony George,

who debuted as Burke in Episode 262
(replacing Mitch Ryan), looks so much

like pre-Guyana Jones they could be twins.

————————————————

"I find the evenings increasingly
tedious of late," says Barnabas,

the crabby vampire, glaring as usual
through an Old House window

frosted with cobwebs—yet another
scene that features his menacing stare

from a darkened window, origin
of the recurring childhood nightmare

in which Barnabas spied me through
my street-facing bedroom window

and broke it with his cane (each time
I woke before he lunged for my neck).

Barnabas's voice drenched in reverb,
Vicki's sour-orange dress, Burke's body

shrouded on the bed—"Keep calm and be
scientific about this," Dr. Hoffman says.

Living off the grid, sort of, in rural
Maine: Dr. Hoffman lights up her

laboratory in the Old House basement
with burning torches on the walls,

but her oscilloscope is useless if it's
not plugged into an electrical socket.

After a week-long break from the poem,
no way I could've prepared for the first

minute of Episode 348: Little David,
the psychic child, sneaks up on Carolyn—

fast asleep under her chartreuse bedspread,
matching pillow propped against plush

aqua headboard, garish orange blanket
rolled at the foot of the bed, a nightshirt

on the verge of pink and teal batik
draped over it—and he stands above

the bed and touches her shoulder as if
she were a strange alien specimen;

thanks, *Dark Shadows*, for reminding me
of three-year-old Ted Bundy creepy-

crawling into his teenage aunt's

bedroom as she took an afternoon

nap and arranging all the kitchen
knives around the bed, the blades

pointing toward her body (I made
a note to research the bed of knives

story, double-check the details
in case my memory was faulty;

channel-surfing just an hour later,
I stumbled on the Bundy documentary

where I originally heard this story,
and—I'm not making this up—

the first scene re-enacted the bed
of knives tale, allowing me to correct

my imprecise first draft, where I'd
written Bundy stalked his sleeping

mother, not his aunt); startled awake,
Carolyn screams and backs away,

prompting Little David's hypnotic,
monotone reply: "I just wanted to make

sure you weren't dead"; don't worry,
Carolyn, that's not a kitchen knife

in the boy's hand, but a grimacing
172-year-old Revolutionary War

toy soldier Ghost Girl gave him
in Episode 331—he's convinced

it will protect you in the spirit world.

———————————————

Dr. Hoffman's experiment fails (next
time, plug in your oscilloscope and nix

the torches on the walls), causing Barnabas
to age decades in one evening, his flesh

withered and desiccated, mouth tucked
into sagging jowls, the vampire stooping

when he tries to stand up straight—
as I might, if I live long enough to watch

all 1,225 episodes and finish this poem.

———————————————————

"A terrible thing can happen—I can't
stop it from happening, I can't do anything,"

says Little David, in a half-fogged
prophecy trance after sneaking up

behind Carolyn again, the glowering
toy soldier pressed against his chest.

Today, an ode to blood: in 1967,
Carolyn's half-drained body—bite

wounds still visible on her neck—
restores Barnabas to middle-age

(a relief for Jonathan Frid, who
endured three hours each morning

in makeup, Styrofoam wrinkles
applied to his face and hands),

and in 1973, Jim Jones, scheming
to move the Peoples Temple out

of the country since his trip to Belo
Horizonte (where Burke Devlin died),

proclaims in righteous preacher bellow,
"My blood is so good—if we could

put it into sick people, they'd be healed."

———————————————————————

"David, you don't want them to send
you away, do you," Carolyn says,

"to a home for mentally disturbed
children"—exactly what my father

used to tell me when I threw a tantrum
(my reply, stuffing temper fits inside,

gunpowder packed into a cannon bore,
known in the *DSM-IV* as Code 300.02,

"Generalized Anxiety Disorder").
Like a conventional soap opera

story arc—Dr. Hoffman planting
an unconscious suggestion in Vicki

to stay away from Barnabas, while
Barnabas in turn drinks Carolyn's

blood, enslaving her, commanding
that she bring Vicki to be his vampire

bride, the new Josette—my childhood
nightmares unfolded in a serial narrative,

three or four times per week, so often
I stopped waking my parents (how could

they, mortals, possibly protect me from
a vampire), and each night Barnabas

got closer, moving from front yard
to roof, then sliding down the shingles

to stare into my bedroom window.

———————————————————————

Roger wants Carolyn to spend some time

In Boston (attend parties with young men

Her own age): it's disturbing, how she pines
On the terrace waiting for the sun to set.

"How long are you going to stand there?"
Carolyn asks Barnabas—pretty nervy,

Getting so impatient with a vampire:
The undead, Carolyn, won't be hurried.

Dr. Hoffman clutches the lab notebook,
Her diary of vampire blood experiments;

A second camera appears, swaying like a cobra,
Nearly bumps into Barnabas and Carolyn.

That death-rattle laugh you hear: Dr. Hoffman
Fleeing from Carolyn at the end of this sonnet

(Sobbing in young lawyer Peterson's office).

———————————————

Sobbing in young lawyer Peterson's office
And swooning when she sees the hypodermic

Syringe that killed Woodard: Dr. Hoffman
Is still haunted by her role in the murder

("No one believes in magic numbers," Carolyn
Says to Barnabas—she's lecturing a dead man

On the occult, a man who sleeps within
A coffin and feeds at night on human

Blood—"next thing, you'll be telling me
You can conjure up a ghost," she laughs).

Dr. Hoffman fumbles with the draperies
In the bedroom, her nerves collapsing;

Off-camera, a stagehand's bawdy whistle
When Carolyn and Lawyer Peterson kiss—

Barnabas, agitated, howling in the distance.

————————————————————

For I consider Lawyer Peterson,
his class antagonism on the prowl,

his feral distrust of the Collins family
and envy for their decadent wealth;

for my first glance at Dr. Hoffman's
cheetah stripes adorning her silk scarf

which she tosses back behind her
shoulder (for then I looked away);

for every gothic tale is incomplete
without a cemetery caretaker who's

mad as a hatter, this one perched
at the Collins tomb like a paranoid

owl tormented by voices of the dead;
for the jumpy dachshund rescued

tonight at my band's rehearsal space—
desk clerk found him in a parked car,

yipping in the December wind-chill;
for I consider my cat, Simon, who

just mounted his brother, Schuster,
bit the back of his neck, held on,

humping next to me on the couch
while I took notes watching the 150th

episode I've seen for this poem.

————————————————————

Trapped an entire episode in her
bedroom with a wicked pack

of cards—windows blow open,
candles go out, dead Dr. Woodard

appears in his burial shroud behind
the curtains, more candles go out,

Woodard's ghost calls on the black
telephone, lights flicker, another ghost

turns the doorknob—Dr. Hoffman
deals herself a game of Solitaire.

Another ghost-call from Woodard
on the black telephone: no one

can stop Dr. Hoffman from turning
every reaction shot into a St. Vitus

Dance of hammed-up twitches,
grimaces, silent-film contortions—

not even Lela Swift, who directed
more episodes of *Dark Shadows*

than anyone else (582, not including
episode 24, mistakenly credited to Swift

but directed by John Sedwick).

————————————————

Revising my Episode 363 notes
into couplets while Johnny Cash's

1969 San Quentin concert played
on the Ovation network (*Carolyn*

accuses Dr. Hoffman of blackmail,
I wrote, *a ruse to hide that she broke*

into Lawyer Peterson's office to steal a diary
for a vampire), I remembered my father

trying to teach me, age seven—two years

after *Dark Shadows* canceled—to play

guitar like Cash, his favorite musician:
"Every time he strums, it sounds like

butter," I said, which was my way
of telling him I couldn't stop listening

to Johnny Cash's guitar; the lessons
ended almost as soon as they began,

my fingers too small to make chords,
he said, but I know it was instead

that familiar queasy feeling, asking
himself why Anthony couldn't just play

"I Walk the Line" without saying
a song is like a dairy product, why

I couldn't be other than his strange son:
"father I am alive!" Frank O'Hara says,

"father / forgive the roses and me."

———————————————

iPod on shuffle, driving home after
band rehearsal, the famously married

indie-pop duo Mates of State came on:
"Nature & the Wreck," from their

Bring It Back album, reminded me,
as I parallel-parked, of making out

on my living room couch with Liz
our first months dating (like teenagers,

we had make-out music, *Bring It Back,*
though sometimes Can's *Tago Mago,*

the CD player locked on repeat);
we met the winter after my marriage

imploded, as I emerged from a month
holed up, Howard-Hughes-like,

in my apartment, watching all four
seasons of *Battlestar Galactica* (but not

spraying the phone, as Hughes did,
for germs), while my cat, Shimmy,

reclined in the crook of my arm
and I ate Grape Nuts with almond

milk every breakfast and dinner—
too lethargic to make anything or

order out, usually skipping lunch,
huddled with this dear animal as if

my apartment were a fallout shelter;
living alone the first time in 15 years,

I forgot how to act in public,
helpless as Ghost Girl fumbling

her lines again tonight, searching
off-camera for cue cards, Barnabas

on his knees, grabbing her shoulders,
saying, "Punish me, Sarah" (and, yes,

his words sounded just as creepy
as you think)—the few times I talked

with anyone, passing neighbors on
the stairs or in the lobby, I forgot

what I wanted to say and my words
came out in halting phrases or manic

paragraphs (Shimmy, my Ghost Cat,
whose ashes sit atop the bookshelf

in a plain white cardboard box
next to her favorite catnip goldfish

and a Saint Francis statue from
psychic Patricia Kennedy, who

called Liz and me the day before
we took Shimmy to the animal

hospital for the last time and said:
"It's not death, honey, you're

freeing her—you're letting her
go to that place where she can

recognize all of her friends").

————————————————

Over 50 hours of my life the last
18 months watching *Dark Shadows,*

yet I'm still surprised when Roger
rakishly sweeps into the drawing room

and says with matter-of-fact aplomb:
"Barnabas, we're going to have another

séance—would you care to join us?"
(what breeze in the Great House

makes Mrs. Stoddard's yellow, puff-
collared Mumu billow, even though

all the doors and windows are shut).
I've been gun-shy, afraid to watch

Episode 366, knowing *Dark Shadows*
is about to time-travel into 1795,

unsure how I'd even begin to write
about an American daytime soap opera

(starring a vampire) that suddenly leaps

backward 172 years but doesn't lose

its audience to *The Edge of Night*
and *You Don't Say!*, its competing

late-1967 shows on CBS and NBC:
we're here now, 1795, and maybe

time-travel is the only narrative
trajectory the show could take

to repress its recent Victorian incest
vibe (running away from the present

to sublimate a taboo): Ghost Girl,
speaking through Vicki in the middle

of the séance, says to her undead
older brother: "Barnabas, when you

marry Josette, will you still *love* me?"

———————————————

I'm as confused as you are, Vicki,
wandering late-eighteenth century

Collinsport like a castaway: my poem
time-travels back to 1795 along with

every actor in *Dark Shadows*, and I
don't know how I'll get used to calling

Ghost Girl "Sarah"; or seeing Joe
in epaulettes as "Navy Lieutenant

Nathan Forbes" instead of Joe who
wears a pea coat and looks like he

beats up hippies; Mrs. Stoddard as
Barnabas's mother, "Naomi Collins";

Burke Devlin (alive again) as "Jeremiah
Collins," Barnabas's uncle and rival

for Josette; or Roger as mutton-
chopped "Joshua Collins," Barnabas's

father, who, like Roger, can't keep
his hands off the sherry decanter.

I've never dared use the word "lugubrious"
in a poem—until now, Joan Bennett

narrating another existentially grim
episode introduction: "That woman

from the present lives in the past
she has always loved," she says of Vicki,

trapped in 1795, "and discovers that our
tragedies often start before we are born"

(the witch Angelique makes her
first appearance since telling me

in a dream 62 episodes ago that coffee
would've protected me from Barnabas

when I was a boy plagued by nightmares).

———————————————

Ghost Girl's Revolutionary War toy soldier
frozen in a grimace: he probably knows

the walls of the Old House will fade over
172 years from pastel pink to Hammer Films

gloom; in 1795, in the witchy hands
of seething Angelique, this harmless little

plaything becomes a voodoo doll
that nearly chokes Barnabas to death.

What passes for advanced medical
science in late-eighteenth-century

rural Maine: "I'm told that Barnabas
was stricken very suddenly, without

any warning whatsoever," the Collins
family doctor says, oddly lapsing into

a slight Scottish accent with every
vowel, "and there is a possibility

he may recover just as suddenly"
(seeing pre-vampiric 1795 Barnabas

powerless, suffocating in his bed,
must have soothed me as a child).

The witch Angelique gathers poisonous
nightshade in a Little Red Riding Hood

wicker basket, claims it's just a bushel
of bay leaves when Collins family servant

Ben Stokes confronts her—she later
enslaves him, just as Barnabas does

to Willie Loomis in 1967—and Lara Parker
reveals in the DVD extras that autograph

seekers followed her to the subway
after show tapings and schoolchildren

were so convinced she was Angelique
they fled to the other end of the platform

when they saw her waiting for a train.

———————————————

Ben Stokes must fetch a spider's web
from an oak tree without breaking

a single thread—is Angelique a witch
or an eighteenth-century Zen master?

With the arrival of an anonymous

bleached-skull wedding gift that terrifies

Josette, a pall descends on Collinwood:
Angelique and Barnabas botch their lines,

another boom-mic shadow flits upon
the wall, Josette fumbles the knob

of Angélique's bedroom door, Kathryn
Leigh Scott's Josette wig exposes

her real hair, the closing theme music
repeats itself like a skipping record,

and yesterday a fly landed on Joshua
Collins's nose (David Trinidad, who

borrowed the first box of DVDs from
the coffin, said last week on the phone:

"When you get to Episode 4"—which
probably won't happen until around 2020—

"your sentence has to be about Joan
Bennett trying to open the parlor door

but it won't give—I watched it five times").
Jeremiah Collins drinks another spiked

toddy, this one tainted with a potion
concocted by Angelique to make him

fall in love with Josette; Barnabas
spends the day patiently tutoring

gentle giant Ben Stokes, unaware
that Angelique cast a spell to make

his bride Josette, in turn, fall for Jeremiah:
"Learning to write is so hard," Ben says,

"I don't know how children do it."

I can't stop myself from rewinding:
Joan Bennett awkwardly tugs the arm

of a mysterious femme fatale
(Josette, of course) kissing Jeremiah

in Naomi Collins's nightmare—then
yanks the woman's arm from her body,

screams at the bloody mannequin
stump in her hands (several frame-

by-frame rewinds, over and over,
watching a stagehand crawl behind

Kathryn Leigh Scott to place the fake
severed arm on Jeremiah's shoulder

as he makes out with Josette/Scott).
Invasive soap opera close-up, just

eyes and cheeks, reveals a star-shaped
mole on Naomi's upper-left cheekbone:

more witchcraft from Angelique,
who branded orphic pitchfork tattoos

on Jeremiah's and Josette's hands
—or is Joan Bennett such a diva

even a fake wart demands "star" treatment?

———————————————

In the middle of another pedantic
monologue from Jeremiah Collins,

the witch Angelique turns his brother,
Joshua, into a black-and-white cat,

Sphinx-reclined on a lace tablecloth
(please don't change Joshua back,

Angelique; I want my memory
of his last words to be the lines

he forgot in mid-sentence the previous
scene: "I heard you say—he was to—

whatever that—vulgar expression was").

———————————————

I'm almost too exhausted to write
a sentence about tonight's episode

("Think of me as a gigantic child,"
Countess du Prés, Josette's mother,

says to Vicki), half-awake and dazed
on the couch, just four hours sleep

last night after taking our cat, Simon,
to Animal 911, the 24-hour pet

hospital, where he was rushed into
emergency surgery for a swollen

bowel; he survived, healing now
on a 10-day antibiotic, and I don't

think I'll forget his plaintive howls
in the living room and pained,

dilated pupils staring at me last
night, his helpless crouch beside

the TV (I slipped the latest *New Yorker*
underneath him as he strained muscles

to shit—fitting, to make a mess of
the *New Yorker* just as the poems do

week after week—but nothing
happened, just Simon flexing his

hindquarters and braying); Liz and I

couldn't believe how quickly Simon

was stricken: I got home from my
night class, The Historical Poem,

a craft seminar on writing extended
archival sequences, and as I took off

my coat, Simon jumped on a cabinet,
shoulder-level with me, and rubbed

madly against the wall, taunting his twin
brother, Schuster; three hours later,

we gave a surgeon permission to cut
into his belly—into a bowel distended

five times its normal size—signing
a "do not resuscitate" order in case

he didn't survive the surgery ("Last time
I came here, I picked up Shimmy's

ashes," Liz said of my Ghost Cat,
to which I replied, "Last time for

me was the day Shimmy died").

————————————————

Josette, when the diabolical Theremin
soundtrack starts playing, you can't

trust that Angelique only wants
to massage your head with rosewater.

An impeccably clumsy return to chroma
key, Barnabas and André (Josette's father)

walking from the dark, late-night
thicket of the Collinwood estate

and emerging—surrounded by
an analog aura, a radioactive glow—

in front of a gigantic, overexposed
stock-photo scrim of a sun-lit

dirt road cutting through a forest.

—————————————————

The bicolor cat turns back into
Joshua—after jealously watching

Naomi drain the sherry decanter—
the night Sandra Simonds and

Joe Harrington read at Columbia
College; after dinner, trying to find

something to sign her credit card
receipt with, Sandra said, "I only have

eyeliner—do you have a pen": David T.
copied her words into his notebook

(like the ones from grade school,
marbled black-and-white cover,

the title *Composition Book* stretched
across the top); I spoke the words

into my phone's Voice Recorder app;
and Joe said, "Everyone at this table

has to write a poem with that line in it."
I've watched so many episodes

(173 since Barnabas rose from
his coffin in the Collins family

tomb) that I recognize the black-
and-green afghan draped across

Jeremiah's and Josette's bewitched
marriage bed at the Collinsport Inn—

the newlyweds still bearing Angelique's
pitchfork tattoos on their hands:

it's the same afghan that, 172 years later,
will decorate the sofa in Sam Evans's

studio, where he paints mawkish
swordfish and tired old men

who look like Norman Mailer.

———————————————————

Barnabas trips over his lines,
nervous about his impending duel

to the death with Jeremiah Collins
("I will be—not sit here accepting this,"

he says, "hating to be with anybody
because I know whoever it is will

be thinking, 'Poor Barnabas'"),
examining his pistol, fingering it

obsessively, rubbing the barrel
to comfort himself—I can't leave

my apartment without checking
and re-checking the oven burners,

embarrassing repetitions that soothe
my fear of surprise catastrophe

long enough for me to walk out the door
and lock it, then I pull the knob at least

four or five times to make sure
it hasn't somehow unlocked itself:

just baffling, an otherwise lucid
adult who believes doors spring

their own locks and faucets turn

themselves on when I walk away.

Vicki is Josef K. trapped in 1795,
badgered by renowned witchfinder

Rev. Trask, a paranoiac straight out
of "The Minister's Black Veil"—

stern forehead and portentous
speech, hands clasped in prayer,

the only character in American soap
history to use the word "abjure"

and expect to be taken seriously.

———————————————

The witch Angelique, trailed by
an oscillating Theremin warble,

casts a spell that kills a tree.

———————————————

Vicki's not a witch, Rev. Trask—
she's just a woman transported

(during a séance) 172 years into
the past to witness the interminable

origin story of the vampire
who will stalk her in the future.

Rev. Trask glowers at Navy Lt.
Nathan Forbes from beneath his

gloomy Bela Lugosi widow's peak:
Trask, witchfinder extraordinaire,

blusters through an exorcism
like he'd rather be doing Reiki.

Children are never safe in *Dark
Shadows*—haunted by witches

and vampires in garrulous, plodding
narrative arcs that take weeks to resolve

(I can't believe I'm still trapped in 1795):
on the shortest day of 1967, the second

Winter Equinox of my life, Angelique
stabs a voodoo needle into the navel

of a scruffy doll that belongs to Sarah
Collins, who will die 26 episodes later—

pneumonia, not Angelique's witchery
—then arise in 172 years to romp

around Collinwood with Little David,
the psychic child ("Afterward, the cradle

rocked itself / for hours," Amy Gerstler
writes in *Ghost Girl*, the book that gave me

a name for Sarah, this poem's Ghost Girl).

———————————————————

Variation on unrequited love in D
minor, watching the next-to-last

episode for Book 1 of this multi-volume
poem that dares me to live long enough

for 1,043 more episodes (ending this
book on a cliffhanger, Barnabas's

unresolved origin story—I've spent
27 episodes in 1795 and he's still not

a vampire): Barnabas is just not that
into you, Angelique, despite your

witchy efforts to woo him—casting
spells on Ben Stokes, Jeremiah,

and Josette; turning Joshua into
a bicolor cat, then back into himself;

afflicting little Sarah with a near-fatal
fever, only to cure her the next day.

Flames crackling behind her
in the Old House fireplace, Naomi

stares at the back of Joshua's head
while Joshua talks to Angelique's neck

as she faces the camera: it's the classic soap
opera shot Liz mentioned 105 episodes ago,

the three arranged in receding perspective, as if
choreographed to form the side of a triangle;

later, real sadness, a sense of loss—I'm
actually finishing Book 1 and don't know

how I'll begin Book 2 (some comfort,
though, when I see the last episode

of Book 1 visually rhyming with the first:
Jeremiah's arm bursts from the soil

of its fresh-dug grave, his hand opens
and closes in a choke-hold, echoing

the closing image of Episode 210,
Barnabas's arm rising from the casket,

free after 172 years, his hand—onyx ring,
ruffled sleeve cuff—gripping like a vise

poor Willie Loomis's windpipe).

Credits

(1967)

Barnabas Collins	Jonathan Frid
Elizabeth Stoddard Collins (Mrs. Stoddard)	Joan Bennett
Roger Collins	Louis Edmonds
Carolyn Collins Stoddard	Nancy Barrett
David Collins ("Little David, the psychic child")	David Henesy
Victoria (Vicki) Winters	Alexandra Moltke
Burke Devlin	Mitch Ryan, Anthony George
Jason McGuire	Dennis Patrick
Willie Loomis	John Karlen
Sam Evans	David Ford
Maggie Evans	Kathryn Leigh Scott
Joe Haskell	Joel Crothers
Dr. Woodard	Robert Gerringer, Peter Turgeon
Dr. Hoffman	Grayson Hall
Sarah Collins ("Ghost Girl")	Sharon Smyth
Sheriff Patterson	Dana Elcar, Angus Cairns
Tony Peterson ("Lawyer Peterson")	Jerry Lacy
Buzz	Michael Hadge
Eagle Hill Cemetery Caretaker	Daniel F. Keyes, Peter Murphy
Mrs. Johnson	Clarice Blackburn

(1795)

Barnabas Collins	Jonathan Frid
Victoria Winters	Alexandra Moltke
Naomi Collins	Joan Bennett
Joshua Collins	Louis Edmonds
Jeremiah Collins	Anthony George
Sarah Collins	Sharon Smyth
Josette du Prés	Kathryn Leigh Scott
André du Prés	David Ford
Countess Natalie du Prés	Grayson Hall
Angelique Bouchard	Lara Parker
Navy Lt. Nathan Forbes	Joel Crothers
Ben Stokes	Thayer David
Rev. Trask	Jerry Lacy

About the Author

Tony Trigilio's most recent books include the poetry collections *White Noise* (Apostrophe Books) and *Historic Diary* (BlazeVOX [books]). He is also the editor of *Elise Cowen: Poems and Fragments* (Ahsahta Press) and author of the critical monograph *Allen Ginsberg's Buddhist Poetics* (Southern Illinois University Press). He directs the program in Creative Writing/Poetry at Columbia College Chicago and co-edits *Court Green*.

25049647R00062

Made in the USA
Charleston, SC
16 December 2013